I0797561

¡Nuestra maravillosa Tierra!
Our Exciting Earth!

MONTAÑAS
MOUNTAINS

Jagger Youssef
traducido por / translated by Eida de la Vega

Please visit our website, www.garethstevens.com. For a free color catalog of all our high-quality books, call toll free 1-800-542-2595 or fax 1-877-542-2596.

Library of Congress Cataloging-in-Publication Data

Names: Youssef, Jagger.
Title: Mountains = Montañas / Jagger Youssef.
Description: New York : Gareth Stevens Publishing, 2018. | Series: Our exciting Earth! = ¡Nuestra maravillosa Tierra! | In English and Spanish. | Includes index.
Identifiers: ISBN 9781538215357 (library bound)
Subjects: LCSH: Mountains–Juvenile literature. Mountain ecology–Juvenile literature.
Classification: LCC GB512.Y68 2018 | DDC 551.43'2–dc23

Published in 2018 by
Gareth Stevens Publishing
111 East 14th Street, Suite 349
New York, NY 10003

Translator: Eida de la Vega
Editorial Director, Spanish: Nathalie Beullens-Maoui
Editor: Therese Shea
Designer: Bethany Perl

Photo credits: Cover, p. 1 Daniel Prudek/Shutterstock.com; pp. 5, 24 VarnaK/Shutterstock.com; p. 7 The World in HDR/Shutterstock.com; p. 9 Sharon Benton/Shutterstock.com; pp. 11, 24 B_Zuber/Shutterstock.com; p. 13 Vitalfoto/Shutterstock.com; p. 15 Ida Viktoria/Shutterstock.com; p. 17 YuriFineart/Shutterstock.com; p. 19 Taras Kushnir/Shutterstock.com; p. 21 luxora/Shutterstock.com; pp. 23, 24 gorillaimages/Shutterstock.com.

Printed in the United States of America

CPSIA compliance information: Batch #CW18GS: For further information contact Gareth Stevens, New York, New York at 1-800-542-2595.

Contenido

Contents

¡Vamos a
las montañas!

Let's go to the
mountains!

Una montaña se eleva sobre la tierra.

A mountain rises above the land.

Una fila de montañas
se llama cordillera.

....

A row of mountains
is a range.

Algunas montañas tienen una cima puntiaguda. A la cima se le llama pico.

....

Some mountains have a pointed top. The top is called a peak.

Hay animales que
viven en las montañas.
¡Veo cabras!

....

Animals live
on mountains.
I see goats!

Las plantas
también crecen ahí.
¡Veo pinos!

....

Plants grow there.
I see pine trees!

Hay gente que
vive ahí. ¡Puede hacer
mucho frío!

....

People live there.
It can be cold!

¡Algunas personas
suben las montañas
a pie!

....

Some people
climb mountains!

Nosotros subimos
en auto.

....

We drive
up a mountain.

Bajamos en esquí.
¡Las montañas
son divertidas!

....

We ski down!
Mountains are fun!

Palabras que debes aprender
Words to Know

(el) pico
peak

(la) cordillera
range

(el) esquí
ski

Índice / Index